T0288406

Play It Safe

CONTENTS

NATIONAL GEOGRAPHIC School Publishing
Hampton-Brown

ai_
_ay

Words with ai, ay

Look at each picture. Read the words.

Example:

ch**ai**n

r**ai**sins

tr**ai**n

h**ay**

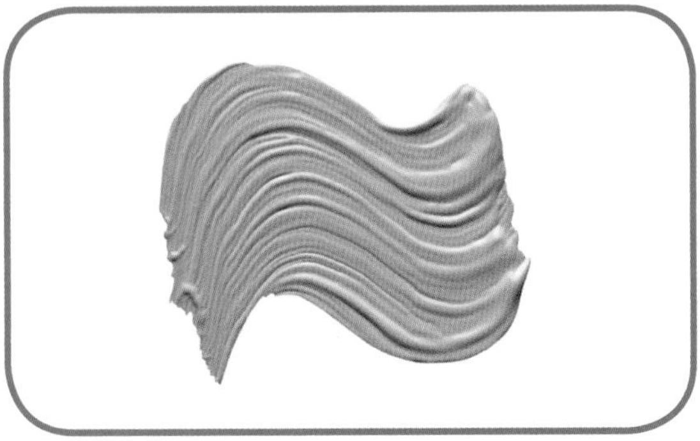

gr**ay**

spr**ay**

High Frequency Words

- about
- don't
- door
- important
- should
- want
- where
- work

Key Words

Read the sentences. Match each sentence to one of the pictures.

Call About Fires Fast!

1. The **door** is on fire!
2. You **should** call for help.
3. **Don't** wait to make an **important** call **about** fire!
4. Tell **where** the fire is.
5. These people **want** to put out the fire.
6. They **work** hard to put out fires.

Why should people call about fires?

Phonics Games

NGReach.com

Help Is on the Way!

by Sterling Spear

Each day firefighters help us. When they get a call about a fire, they do not wait. They run to the fire truck.

The wailing fire truck races to the fire. If you see it, step back. Firefighters have to get to the fire fast. Stay out of the way!

Firefighters don't delay. It is important to see if people need help. They must put out the fire. They may need to rescue people.

Firefighters are brave. They risk their lives aiding the public. People say they trust firefighters to help them.

A firefighter's work is hard. As a rule, people who want to be firefighters must pass lots of tests. They should be fit and strong. So they train a lot.

These firefighters are at a training class. Look at the details in this snapshot. That is a big hose. Firefighters should be strong to spray the water.

Firefighters help each other. Fighting fires is a big job. These firefighters need each other to spray water on the flames.

When a home is on fire, firefighters may need to go inside. They know just what to do if a door is closed. They think fast. This firefighter chopped down the door with an ax.

This firefighter went inside to save people. If people can't escape the fire, they may be in pain. They may have fainted. Maybe they can't walk yet. Firefighters save people. That is their job.

They save pets, too. This cat was in a home when it was on fire. The firefighter came to its aid. He saved the cat from the thick, gray smoke.

When there is no fire, firefighters work to maintain their equipment. They have to be set to go. They have an important job. Do you want to be a firefighter some day?

Words with ai, ay

Read these words.

day	wait	flames	rescue	wailing
aid	spray	gray	fire	pet

Find the words with **ai** or **ay**.
Use letters to build them.

d a y

Talk Together

Choose words from the box above to tell your partner what the people do.

Syllable Division

Look at each picture. Read the words.

paper

cabin

photo

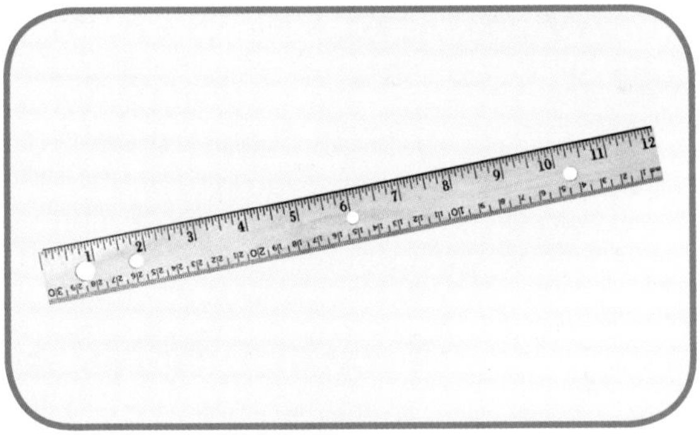

ruler

tiger

radish

High Frequency Words
about
don't
door
important
should
want
where
work

Key Words

Read the sentences. Match each sentence to one of the pictures.

Know About Fires

1. It's **important** to know what to do in a fire.
2. You **should work** on an escape plan.
3. **Don't** open a hot **door**, even if you **want** to get out.
4. If you can't get out, it's important to yell for help.
5. Tell **about** the fire and **where** it is.

Phonics Games
NGReach.com

Don't Panic, Be Safe

by Lorna Shore
illustrated by Jennifer Zivoin

Here is an important rule. Never play with matches or fire. Little fires get big fast! A fire can make a home vanish. Here are some things you can do to be safe.

If you see a fire, don't panic! Get away from the fire. Then call for help. A fire is a crisis. It's important! Lives may depend on you.

In lots of places, you can call 911. Do not panic. Do not yell. Tell the important details. Tell where the fire is. Tell what you see. Stay on the phone in case you can help.

Wait for the firefighters to come. Stand back. They need lots of space to work. You will be safe, too. In a fire, things can fall or explode.

Do you know what to do in the event of a fire at home? Work with your family to make an escape plan. Have fire drills so you know the plan well. Pick a place outside to gather and wait for each other.

If there's a fire in your home, you must go outside to get away. But before you open a door, check to see if it is hot. Never open hot doors! Never open a door if smoke is coming under it.

If you can’t get out, open a window.
Smash it if you must. Yell, “Help! Fire!”

Use the plan your family made to escape. Stay close to the floor if there is a lot of smoke. Exit the moment you can.

Go to the gathering place. Do not panic. Stand back from the fire. Wait for the firefighters to come. They can help your family.

Don't go back inside even if your family pets are missing. Tell the firefighters about them. They rescue pets, too.

Here are the rules. Don't panic. Never play with fire. You may save your life and your family. ❖

Syllable Division

Read these words.

open	escape	place	lives	go
crisis	exit	moment	vanish	panic

Find the words with more than one syllable. Use letters to build them.

o p e n

Talk Together

Choose words from the box above to tell your partner what the people should do.

Exit the moment you can.

Fire! Don't Delay!

Help the fire truck drive to the fire fast. Trace the path with your finger. The sentences tell you where to go.

1. Pass the hotel with gray rails.
2. Go up at the grain silo. It's important!
3. You should drive over railway tracks.
4. You'll want to pass the gray clay snail.
5. Don't pass the men painting a door! If you do, you may vanish in a radish patch!
6. Take the path to the cabin.
7. Work with the men spraying water!

Acknowledgments
Grateful acknowledgment is given to the authors, artists, photographers, museums, publishers, and agents for permission to reprint copyrighted material. Every effort has been made to secure the appropriate permission. If any omissions have been made or if corrections are required, please contact the Publisher.

Photographic Credits
CVR Kayte Deioma/PhotoEdit. **2** (bl) ryasick photography/Shutterstock. (br) Jupiterimages. (cl) Mikael Damkier/Shutterstock. (rcb, tl) PhotoDisc/Getty Images. (rct) ZTS/Shutterstock. **3** Liz Garza Williams/Hampton-Brown/National Geographic School Publishing. **4** image100/ SuperStock. **5** Clint Hild/iStockphoto. **6** Slobo Mitic/iStockphoto. **7** Code Red/Collection Mix: Subjects/Getty Images. **8** Mark Richards/PhotoEdit. **9** David Duprey/AP Images. **10** MISHELLA/Shutterstock. **11** Charles O'Rear/Corbis. **12** JGI/Getty Images. **13** The York Dispatch, Jason Plotkin/AP Images. **14** Juan Carlos Ulate/Reuters/Corbis. **15** Liz Garza Williams/Hampton-Brown/National Geographic School Publishing. **16** (bl) Digital Vision/ Getty Images. (br) Constant/Shutterstock. (cl) STOCKbeeld/Alamy Images. (cr) Getty Images. (tl) Shawn Gearhart/iStockphoto. (tr) Michael Shake/Shutterstock. **17** Liz Garza Williams/ Hampton-Brown/National Geographic School Publishing. **29** Liz Garza Williams/Hampton-Brown/National Geographic School Publishing.

Illustrator Credits
3, **15**, **17**, **29** Peter Grosshauser; **18-28** Jennifer Zivoin; **30-31** Jannie Ho

National Geographic School Publishing
Hampton-Brown
www.NGSP.com

Printed in the USA.
Quad Graphics, Leominster, MA

ISBN:978-0-7362-8068-6

18 19
10 9 8 7